CONTENTS

A Little About the Author

To tell you about my background, you might think I am an odd choice of a person to write this book. First of all, I did not go to college for business or anything else that would make me any sort of an "expert". I went to college to be an EMT, yep, not what you expected is it? Like many people, my plans, circumstances and life goals changed that. I worked some jobs that made me unhappy while I was trying to figure out how to have the kind of life that I would enjoy. I have always been artsy and come from a family of woodworkers. I have tried many times in the past to make and sell things. I always knew that I could definitely be happy if I was able to make at least enough money to live off of by doing this. A couple problems always stood in my way, Time and Money! I am gonna go out on a limb here and guess that at least half of the people reading this book have some similarities to this little story.

And then Covid hit. Most people took an even harder look on their lives and careers during this time. I was no exception. I decided what I wanted most was to work for myself. This was both a good and bad time to start this journey. The down side was most people were not going anywhere. They were also not shopping for things at boutiques or craft fairs or the normal places that someone would sell handmade items, except for online. While the internet seemed like a great place to sell, and it is, it also was a bit intimidating for me just starting.

I started planning and researching and trying to learn as much as I could about how to make my dream come true. I also started small and bought a cricut. I thought that this was going to be the difference I needed. Well, so did everyone else that was stuck in their houses with a cricut during covid. But I decided to diversify. I also became an Ordained Minister. Super easy to do online for a small fee. But, covid meant no weddings were happening. Why are you reading a book written by an idiot? Well, maybe it's because I hopefully, eventually, figured this mess out. Spoiler alert, I did figure it out, eventually. But while I was trying to get it all together, I turned to being a delivery driver for doordash, uber, grubhub, instacart, amazon flex and walmart's spark. Glamorous, isn't it? What that did do for me is create the freedom and cash that I needed to solve those annoying time and money problems that I was unable to shake with my 9 to 5. Downside to this is the inconsistency in paychecks and the wear and tear on your vehicle. Owning your own business definitely will not give you consistent paychecks, but it is more stable than relying on apps that can crash or other outside forces that you have little control over. Long story short, I still wanted to get out of this eventually or at least have it become just a filler during slow times.

I kept learning. I kept scouring the internet for all the wisdom I could absorb. I joined facebook groups for everything from becoming an entrepreneur to lasers for beginners. It is amazing how much you can learn from those groups. I also attended Youtube University almost religiously, no pun intended on the reverend status I had obtained along the way. But by the end of this, most of which took place in between delivering burgers and groceries, I learned quite a bit. I am now the owner of a business that does fairly well. I learned how to start with nothing and turn it into what I had always dreamed of. Then I thought, maybe I should save some people a little time and just put it all together so they can do it faster than I did.

Some of this book will be the boring stuff that is, frankly, not at all fun. If you are wanting to start a business, that is just how it goes. Not everything about owning a business is fun. Personally, I absolutely hate the desk work side of things and would much rather just be making things all day. I also hate trying to figure out pricing and worry that it will not be good enough or too expensive. This is a stressful part to navigate. I am really hoping that I can answer all of that for you and more.

CHAPTER 1: INTRO TO A BUSINESS WITH A LASER

Starting a small business can be an exciting and rewarding endeavor. Using a laser can make manufacturing more products and growing as a company much easier and faster. With the ability to create unique and customizable products, you have the potential to stand out in a crowded market.

In this chapter, I'll introduce you to the basics and key steps of starting a business with a laser engraving and cutting machine. Later chapters will elaborate on these topics. This is just more or less the outline of what we will be talking about, along with some of the very first steps to creating the foundation of a business. So even though this chapter is packed with information that is very useful, it's the boring stuff.

A solid business plan is essential to your success as it outlines your goals and strategies for achieving them. Your business plan should include a company description, market analysis, financial projections, and marketing plan. Even if the plan is only used to set goals for yourself, it's still a good foundation to build from. If you search about how to write a business plan, it will most likely come up with something that is very long and time consuming. You can make one with extensive detail or maybe just a few sentences to set some framework for what your vision is and the goals you have for yourself.

Establishing a budget and managing cash flow is crucial to keeping your business afloat. Make sure you have a system for tracking your expenses, revenue, and profits. Whatever system works best for you. It may be hard at first to determine your average monthly expenses and income. Some of this will just come over time as you learn more about the costs of things.

Prioritize your expenses so you know what is essential and what can be cut in case of financial difficulties. Track your spending to stick to your budget. You can use accounting software, such as QuickBooks or even systems like Square, to monitor expenses, enter invoices, record payments, and reconcile bank accounts. Keeping track of your spending will help you adjust your budget in real-time and avoid overspending. It will also be crucial at tax time for deductions.

Quick and efficient invoicing ensures your clients pay you on time and send reminders to clients. It's crucial to establish payment terms to ensure you receive payment within a reasonable timeframe. Also, if it is a large customized piece, you will definitely want payment up front. Hoping to not have them back out and leave you with items that you can't sell to anyone else is not the way to go.

Keep a close eye on your inventory to avoid overspending on materials or wasted inventory from product expiration or obsolescence. Keep a reserve fund or line of credit available in case of emergencies. This will provide a safety net in case of unexpected expenses or revenue shortfalls.

Review your budget monthly and adjust if necessary. This will allow you to stay on top of expenses and adjust your strategies accordingly.

Determine the legal structure of your business, whether it's a sole proprietorship, partnership, LLC, or corporation, and register your business with the state. Registering your business will help you get a tax ID number, which you will need to have at most locations where you plan to sell your goods. You can easily do this by either going to your state's department of revenue site online or by making a phone call to them. There will also be additional information that will be worth your time to read or ask about when you are there registering. There are several types of business legal structures, each with its own benefits. Here are some common business legal structures and their advantages:

- Sole Proprietorship: It is the simplest and most common legal structure. A sole proprietorship is an unincorporated business that is owned by one person. It's easy to set up and manage, and the owner has complete control over the business. Additionally, the owner is only taxed on the profits of the business. However, the owner is also personally liable for the business's debts and legal issues.

- Partnership: It's a legal structure that features two or more co-owners, where each partner contributes capital and shares profits and losses. Partnerships are relatively simple to establish, and each partner has no personal liability for the debts of other partners. However, partners are jointly liable for the debts of the partnership.

- Limited Liability Company (LLC): It combines the simple management of a partnership with the benefits of limited liability protection. LLC owners, known as members, are not personally liable for the company's debts and legal issues. An LLC also offers flexibility in tax treatment, as it can be set up as a sole proprietorship, partnership, or corporation for tax purposes.

- Corporation: It's a legal structure that treats the business as a separate entity from the owners. Shareholders own the corporation and have limited liability protection. Corporations have more complex tax requirements and are subject to regulation. However, they also offer many benefits, such as greater access to capital, stability, and the potential for more significant growth.

- Cooperative: A cooperative is a business structure owned and operated by a group of members who share values and work together towards a common goal. The members pool their resources to produce and sell goods and services. Members elect a board of directors to manage the business. Cooperatives operate on a democratic principle, where members have an equal say in decision-making.

You may need to obtain permits and licenses to operate your business legally. Check with your local government to see what is required. Also, business insurance can be very helpful. Some venues or events that you sell at may even require you to have it. Business insurance is typically very affordable and easy to obtain.

Establish a brand identity that reflects your business's values and target audience. This includes creating a logo, website, and social media presence. If you need help with a logo and branding for your business, there are some places you can go to for help with those things. Freelance designers are a great way to get high-quality logo designs and branding at an affordable price. You can find freelance designers on websites such as Upwork, Fiverr, and 99designs. You can browse their portfolio and reviews and find the one that is the right fit for your business. Design agencies can offer comprehensive branding solutions, including logo design, branding, and marketing strategies. Design agencies can be expensive, but they can offer more in-depth and tailored branding services. Online logo makers are another way to create your logo. These websites usually offer a wide selection of logos for you to choose from, or you can create your own design. Some popular online logo makers include LogoMaker, Canva, and Wix Logo Maker. If you are short on a budget, you can also do it yourself.. Basically, there are several options to get help with a logo and branding. Consider your budget and the level of expertise required and find a solution that is best for your business.

Develop a marketing strategy to promote your business.

Identify your target audience. This was mentioned above but I will elaborate quickly. What I mean is, do you want to sell trending items to all of suburbia, quirky, fun, one off items, kids themed things, holiday products, men's items and accessories, or something else entirely. As you can imagine from that short list, different types of people are interested in different items and styles. They also tend to shop at different locations and in different ways. So knowing who you will be selling to will help you learn what, how and where to sell it.

Build a content strategy, and leverage social media and other digital platforms. Marketing and advertising is your friend. By defining your target market, you can tailor your marketing efforts to reach the right audience and increase your chances of converting those leads into customers.

Research your industry, competitors, and customers to understand their preferences, needs, and behaviors. Look at demographic data such as age, gender, location, education, income, and lifestyle. Study the demographics and behavior of your current customers to identify any patterns. This can help you understand your target market and identify opportunities to target more of those customers. Consider their preferences, needs, and pain points and build your marketing strategy to address them. Reach out to people in your target market and gather feedback. This can help you understand their preferences and needs. Evaluate your product or service offerings to identify which groups of customers they cater to. This can help you identify any gaps in your product offerings that may appeal to an untapped market.

Once you've identified your target market, you can tailor your marketing efforts to address their pain points and capture their attention. It is crucial to create a marketing strategy that resonates with your target market and showcases how your product or service can help solve their problems. With a focused strategy, you can connect with your target market and build a loyal customer base that drives your business forward.

Pain points in marketing refer to the challenges or issues that customers face, which prompt them to seek a solution. Some common ones include:

-Lack of awareness, many customers may not know about a particular product or service. Especially new and different ideas.

-High prices: Customers may feel that a product or service is too expensive and look elsewhere.

-Poor quality: Customers may have experienced poor quality products or services in the past.

-Complicated purchasing process: Customers may find the purchasing process to be too complicated or overly time-consuming.

-Poor customer service: Customers may have had bad experiences with customer service in the past. If they have to wait for answers to questions or if they don't feel respected, they will leave.

-Lack of trust: Customers may not trust a particular brand or company.

-Inconvenient location: Customers may find a store or service to be too far away or not easily accessible.

By addressing these pain points, marketers make their products or services seem more appealing to potential customers and improve their overall marketing strategies. Not only will you want to keep these things in mind while starting and operating your business. You may want to use the negative side of other companies and products to show how much better your products and company are to work with.

As your business grows, you may need to hire employees or freelancers. Hire people who share your vision and values and have the skills to help your business succeed. Hiring employees is an essential aspect of a company's growth and success.

Most often the people you hire at first will be friends and family. Maybe you will want to keep it that way, which is completely fine. But for those who don't necessarily or can't find the right people within that group, here is a quick guide to what you should know about having employees. It's not just about finding the right person - there are many legal considerations, management responsibilities, and financial implications you need to keep in mind. Hire employees in accordance with employment laws and regulations. This includes compliance with anti-discrimination laws, minimum wage laws, overtime pay laws, and other legal requirements. Make sure to review and follow all applicable federal and state employment laws. Write clear and concise job descriptions and include essential skills and required education. This will help you narrow down candidates' expectations and help you find the right fit. Develop a clear, consistent, and fair hiring process that includes a job application form, resume review, interviews, pre-employment testing, and reference checks. Create an effective onboarding process that includes training, orientation, and paperwork completion.

Most likely this next portion will take some time to get set up and depending on your business structure, may never apply to you. Determine what benefits and compensation package you will offer that is in line with industry standards. This includes benefits such as health insurance, retirement plans, vacation time, and sick leave. Develop a process to evaluate employees' performance and provide feedback on their performance. This can include setting goals and expectations, providing regular feedback, and conducting performance reviews. Develop strategies to retain your employees, such as providing opportunities for career advancement, competitive salaries and benefits, and ongoing training and professional development. Keep in mind that hiring employees is a significant responsibility that requires careful consideration and planning. Building a strong team is critical to the success of your business. Make sure to take the time to find the right people, set expectations, provide training and feedback, and offer competitive compensation.

Be open to pivoting your business as necessary. Sometimes, the business landscape changes, and you may need to adapt your strategies to stay competitive. Starting a business is a significant undertaking. Keeping some of these key things in mind can help you establish a strong foundation for your business's success.

Once you have your business foundation in place, it is time to figure out the products. The first thing you need to do is research and choose the right laser engraving and cutting machine for your needs. Consider the size of the machine, the power of the laser, and the materials you plan to work with. In the next chapter we will get into the many options that are out there for lasers. They vary widely in what they can do and the cost of the different machines.

Choose your products. The versatility of a laser allows you to create a wide range of products, from custom signs and jewelry to personalized gifts and home decor. It is best to do your research for what is selling best in your area, what is currently trending and if there is a niche that is not being filled that you are interested in. We will dive into this much more later in the book.

Find reliable suppliers for your materials and supplies. Be sure to research the quality of the materials, the cost, and the availability. If your lead times are too long that will be a problem. If your materials are subpar, you might not get the prices you want regardless of the efforts you put in. Keep in mind also that your cost per item needs to include any tax and shipping costs to you. There are ways to set up purchases through some suppliers so that you don't pay tax on your blank materials. If you are buying in bulk from wholesalers and you are intending to change the product and then resell it, there are tax laws that keep you from needing to pay taxes on some of what you buy. This could be worth digging into and asking about. You will want to factor these extra costs into your overall costs of making the product. Develop a pricing strategy that considers the cost of your materials, the time it takes to produce each item, and your profit margins. Nobody goes into business just to break even.

Create memorable designs using the appropriate software for your machine. This can include Adobe Illustrator, CorelDRAW, and AutoCAD. You can also find images available online in many locations that we will discuss later. If you are going to be selling the goods you are making, you will want to be sure that you have commercial licensing rights to any images used. This is not as complicated as it sounds, I promise.

Build a strong online presence through social media and e-commerce platforms, such as Etsy or your own website, to showcase your products and attract customers. We will get into other options and pros and cons to those later.

Attend craft fairs and other local events to showcase your products in person and gain exposure. Nothing is better than getting your products into the hands of potential customers. Often people like to see what they are getting before they buy. Also it can be incredibly beneficial to observe customer reactions to various products. Which ones are drawing their attention. Is it also in part because of product placement? There is so much that can be gained by watching and taking note of what people are liking.

Learn how to manage your businesses finances, taxes, and expenses. This is one of the least fun but most critical things to do correctly as a new business owner. Most businesses that fail do so because of financial reasons. It doesn't matter how good your ideas are if you can't make them work long term.

Scaling your business, adding new products, and exploring new markets are essential for long-term business growth and success. Markets are forever changing and evolving, and you need to too. What is trending today, this week, or this month, might not sell at all next month. Also remember that when you are buying materials. Don't go overboard getting supplies until you know what will actually sell.

A new small business with a laser engraving and cutting machine can be challenging but rewarding. Make sure to carefully research and plan before diving in headfirst. This can get very expensive very fast. However, with the correct gear, processes, and marketing strategies, your business can thrive. It is a great way to create unique and customized products quickly and efficiently. The rest of this book will be full of ideas and information that can help you turn your dreams into reality and be successful long term. So if not everything applies to your situation, skip over and then go back to this book again over time as a reference when things pop up. If things are not quite working the way you had in mind, maybe you can try a different strategy that we will talk about. There is no way to just write a step by step process that will work for everyone or every business.

CHAPTER 2: CHOOSING A LASER

A good place to start is figuring out what laser is best for your needs. In this chapter, we'll explore different types of lasers to help you choose the one that's right for you. Some common types of lasers are CO2, fiber and diode.. They vary widely with their uses and capabilities. You might not be able to fully make this decision until you decide on the products you want to make and other factors. But I am going to get into the differences now so that you can keep it in mind when thinking about where you want to start on this journey. Most likely cost will be the biggest factor. However, if you already have a very specific idea, then most often, a certain type of laser will be a better fit than others for what you are doing.

CO2 Lasers are the most common type used for engraving and cutting. They use a gas mixture to produce a continuous laser beam. They can engrave and cut a variety of materials, including wood, acrylic, fabric, leather, and more. CO2 lasers are available in different wattages, typically ranging from 30W to 150W. The price for CO2 lasers can range from around $2,500 to over $10,000 depending on the size and wattage of the machine.

Many people choose CO2 lasers because they have very high precision. They can perform high precision cutting and engraving tasks with accuracy down to 0.001 inches. They are also very versatile. They are capable of handling a wide range of materials, including wood, plastic, glass, metal, and more. In a business where time is money, the high speed of CO2 lasers make them ideal for mass production and high-volume manufacturing. They are also low maintenance and have a longer lifespan compared to other types of laser machines.

The downside is, they are expensive. They also have limited thickness capacity compared to other types of laser machines, so they may not be suitable for thicker materials. They can also suffer from output issues. CO_2 lasers have a limited output and can be impacted by the consistency and quality of the beam output. In addition to those things there are also safety concerns: CO_2 laser machines require proper safety protocols to ensure the protection of operators and others nearby. They can also produce hazardous fumes during cutting and engraving, requiring additional safety precautions.

Next up, fiber lasers. These lasers use an optical fiber doped with rare-earth elements like erbium, ytterbium, or neodymium to create a high-powered, focused beam. They are often used for metal engraving and cutting, including stainless steel, aluminum, and brass. Fiber lasers are available in different wattages, typically ranging from 10W to 100W for cutting and 20W to 50W for engraving. The price for fiber lasers can range from around $5,000 to over $50,000 depending on the size and wattage.

Fiber lasers are fast. They are known for their high-speed cutting and engraving capabilities. They can perform large-volumes of work in a fraction of the time compared to other types of lasers. Fiber lasers also can cut and engrave materials with superior precision, offering accuracy of up to 0.0001 inches. They have a long lifespan and require minimal maintenance compared to other types of laser machines. Also, fiber lasers have a high energy efficiency, meaning they consume less energy to operate than other types of lasers.

Now for the cons, fiber lasers cost much more than CO_2 or diode lasers. While fiber lasers can cut and engrave a wide range of materials, they may not be suitable for some specialized materials. They work best on metal, plastic, and composite materials. They also require water cooling systems to operate. This can increase their overall cost and make installation more complicated. They also can produce toxic fumes during cutting and engraving, requiring special precautions and adequate ventilation.

Finally diode lasers: These lasers use a semiconductor that basically is a one way switch to direct current to produce a focused beam of light. They are often used for small-scale engraving and marking. Diode lasers are available in lower wattages, usually ranging from 2W to 20W for engraving, and the price for a diode laser can range from around $500 to $5,000 depending on the wattage.

Diode lasers are relatively affordable compared to other types of lasers. They are a popular choice for small businesses and hobbyists. They offer high energy efficiency, meaning they consume less energy to operate than other types of lasers. They are compact, portable and lightweight, making them convenient for mobile customization. Diode lasers can also cut and engrave a wide range of materials such as wood, acrylic, leather, and fabric.

The downside to diode lasers is that they have limited power output compared to other types of lasers, making them unsuitable for some heavy-duty applications. They also have a shorter lifespan compared to fiber and CO2 lasers. They are not suitable for cutting through thick materials like metal. Diode lasers require more maintenance than other types of laser machines due to their components' sensitivity to dust and dirt.

It's important to note that while CO2 and fiber lasers are capable of both engraving and cutting, diode lasers are generally only used for engraving. They can however cut through thinner softer materials. Additionally, the cost of the laser machine is not the only factor to consider - you may also need to budget for additional software, accessories, and maintenance costs. It's important to carefully consider your needs and budget before making a purchase decision.

Above, we touched on safety issues with the different types of lasers. I think it is important to point out some of those in more detail. Not only should you be aware of them for your own benefit but some of the hazards require you to purchase added safety equipment.

First and foremost, lasers can cause permanent damage to the eyes if they are directed towards them. This can lead to vision loss, eye pain, and even blindness. You should never look directly at a laser beam. Some lasers come equipped with a shield or tinted protective glass or plastic to look through while it is operating. If the laser you are looking at is an open plane style and does not have this feature, consider getting it as an add on or even special safety glasses for all people to wear when they are in the room with a laser during its operation.

Lasers can also cause skin damage if they are directed towards the skin. This can lead to burns, scarring, and other skin problems. Make sure that you do not put your hands near a laser while it is running. There are many different ways to clamp or magnet down materials so you don't have to physically touch it during operation.

Another big issue is the fire danger. Lasers can be a fire hazard if they are used improperly or if they come into contact with flammable materials. Many people use them to cut or engrave wood. Obviously, wood is flammable. There are ways to adjust your power, speed and even air assist settings that greatly reduce your risk of a fire. However, the danger is always there. Inconsistencies or even glues or additives that you may not even think of in the materials can cause it to flame up at any given time. Lasers should never be left unattended during operation. Not only can fires cause permanent damage to the machine itself, but it can also burn down your house or business if not caught early. You should always have a fire extinguisher or other fire suppression gear readily available.

Another risk is electrical shock. It might be a less likely problem but if they are not used properly or if they are damaged, the risk is definitely there.

Some lasers use chemicals that can be hazardous if they are not handled properly. This can lead to chemical burns, respiratory problems, and other health issues.

As with almost everything in this world, it is important to follow proper safety protocols and to use appropriate protective equipment when working with lasers.

Now for a less dark topic, accessories! Typically lasers come very bare bones. Some companies offer some very cool bundles but not all of them do. Thinking about what you might want to make with your laser ahead of time will help with deciding which one to get and what to get with it.

If you are going to be doing some cutting. First of all it can't just sit on your kitchen table and be good to go. You will need a steel plate bottom so that the power of the laser doesn't cut into your furniture.

Speaking of cutting, you can't lay a piece of wood down onto that steel plate and expect the laser to cut through it cleanly without a fire. It will need to be raised up with some honeycomb or triangular prisms. This is a matter of preference and some people, myself included, alternate between them depending on the job and the size of the pieces or even the type of material. They each have pros and cons. Honeycomb for example, if it isn't big enough for the job you are doing, it won't help. Make sure you buy the biggest one that your laser can use so you are able to use it as often as possible. They are much better for keeping small pieces in place after they fall so that the laser head doesn't hit a tipped up little bit and jar your entire project. They also work great for using push pins or magnets to secure the corners of the material so it stays in place. If your material blows around, your project will inevitably be ruined.

This brings me to an air assist. These are incredibly handy. They help create a much cleaner cut and keep soot from lining the edges of the project. Overall leaving you with a much nicer finished product. There are times when you will not want to turn it on but most times you will be very happy you made that investment and use it often, I'm sure.

Something else that can be crucial is an air purifying system or a vacuum system to pull fumes away. There are so many options and most are very dependent on the laser choice that you make. But keep it in mind because as you know, fumes are a problem.

There are also fun attachments such as rotary tools. There are variations with these as well that work with different size materials and different lasers. Typically you will want to see if there is one meant for your particular laser. If not you will want to make sure it will connect to the laser and the operating program for it.

Knowing what you want to make and the volume you expect to produce will help greatly in making your purchases. So far the dollar signs are adding up, I know. But with the right products and a little planning and experience, you will be making a profit before long. Many people start small and work their way up. With just a couple thousand dollars you really can get all the things you need to produce enough inventory to head out to your first craft show and start making some of that money back. Then just keep reinvesting. Before you know it, and I mean that, you will be talking about getting a bigger and better laser. With that being said, if you can afford it from the jump, you might want to take the leap right away.

CHAPTER 3: CHOOSING YOUR PRODUCTS

This can be both fun and stressful. You want to make sure you make the right choice but you also have so many ideas and might want to try them all. If you have come this far, I am sure you have already seen enough products that have caught your attention. You could probably add several items to what I am going to list in this chapter. If not, then I am not sure why you made it this far into this book. This industry needs people to keep coming up with new and different ideas that will keep things exciting for all of us makers as well as our customers. So please don't take this chapter as a full and complete list of what can be done. I am only briefly touching on the ideas to show how diverse it can be. I am very much looking forward to one day seeing ads or stores full of the great things that you come up with.

I am going to start with a little PSA on safety and get that out of the way. There are some problematic materials out there. Some are difficult to work with and some are dangerous. I will point out the safety concerns here so that we can all keep them in mind. They can impact you, your family, or the environment. Some of these materials should never be used, some you just need to be careful with and others are just simply very tricky..

-Reflective materials: Laser beams can be reflected off of certain materials and cause harm, so it is important to avoid using reflective materials such as metals or mirrors. There are ways to process these materials safely with other added steps. A painted surface will definitely help on metal and a mirror must be engraved from the back, but obviously you also need to "mirror" the image as well.

-Transparent materials: Transparent materials such as glass or plastic can also be hazardous when used with lasers because they can focus the laser beam and cause damage. Just like the metal and mirror, it is possible to use these but you won't have any luck with them without adding other materials. Mostly the beam will just pass through and not do much if anything. They make special paper that can be put on the bottom side and then you would "mirror" that image also. There are also ways to mix up a thinned out paint mixture that would be washed off after processing. Youtube will be very handy here.

-Flammable materials: Lasers can ignite flammable materials such as paper, wood, or fabrics. If I tried to tell you not to use any wood, you would probably stop reading right here. Obviously it is one of the most used materials in lasers. So yes, it definitely can be done safely. You need to be mindful of your settings and do a test run with that type of wood you will be using in your laser (while watching closely of course) to see how your laser performs. They make test grids that you can upload or make your own. Essentially it is a chart that slowly increases the power along one of the axes and slowly increases or decreases speed along the other. That will help you to establish correct settings for that material and your laser. This will also show you when it is too much power and running too slow, be ready to put out the flames.

-Toxic materials: Lasers can cause toxic materials such as certain plastics or metals to release harmful fumes or dust, so it is important to handle these materials with care and in a well-ventilated area. Always do your research on materials before you use them. Certain paints, or other chemical coatings are very bad for your health and the environment.

-Biological materials: Lasers can cause damage to living tissues, so it is important to avoid directing lasers towards people or animals. I really wish that wasn't a sentence that needed to be added here. I feel like if you bought this book to try to learn about this journey before taking the leap, you most likely have enough common sense to not put your hand into a laser. With that being said, accidents do happen and we all probably have at least one dumb friend. Keep them away.

As with just about everything, it is important to read the manufacturer's instructions carefully and to follow all safety protocols to prevent harm to yourself and others.

Back to the fun stuff. It's time to decide what products you'll be offering. We will touch on different types of products, how to research the market demand for them, and how to choose the right products for your business.

As we already know, a laser can be used to create a wide range of products, limited only by your imagination, the materials you have on hand, and the capabilities of your specific laser machine. Here are some examples of products that can be created with a laser:

-Personalized items: you can do this to all kinds of things such as keychains, bookmarks, phone cases, jewelry, home decor, or even things like guns. You can put names or monograms on just about anything.

-Signs: you can create welcome signs, wall art, and decor, including wooden plaques, acrylic or glass signs, and more. The possibilities here are endless. These are one of the main things you will see being made. They can be engraved or cut out or both with layers.

-Jewelry and Accessories: A laser can be used to engrave and cut unique patterns or designs into materials like leather, wood, and acrylic to create custom jewelry and accessories, such as bracelets, necklaces, earrings, and keychains. Who doesn't love to get one of a kind jewelry?

-Home Goods: A laser can be used to create custom home goods, such as coasters, cutting boards, and serving trays, as well as personalized gifts like mugs or wine glasses. This is incredibly popular.

-Holiday decorations: anything from custom tree ornaments to wreaths to hanging halloween decorations to centerpieces. Your imagination can run wild here and people really love changing things up for the holidays. Also a fun idea is things that you can cut out that kids can paint and assemble to give as gifts also.

-Promotional items: bulk things for your business or for other businesses, or fundraising events. You can save money on advertising for yourself. You can also make good money in a short time with laser production runs and bulk rates for other organizations. If you want to work smarter and not harder, it is something you will really want to consider. Some ideas are pens, tumblers, usb drives, business cards, to just name a few.

-Packaging and Labels: A laser can also be used to create custom packaging and labels, including branded boxes, gift tags, and product labels. Here we go putting the paper in the laser. But, yes, it does work and can be very handy and save lots of money.

-Fabric and Clothing: The laser can also cut fabric and can be used to etch or engrave designs on fabric. Remember, your safety warnings here as well. But some of the leather and denim looks with lasers are so amazing. Even if this isn't your main area, you might want to at least play with this at some point.

-Speaking of Leather: wallets, handbags, belts are just a few more options. I'm sure I don't need to mention hat patches.

-Wedding Decor: I will not list all the possibilities in this category but if you had a laser and a cricut with a few other tools, you could do an entire wedding I am pretty sure.

-Electronics: Yep, you can even engrave your laptop, tablet, phone, gaming system. Not only can it add some of your style it also will help make it very identifiable. It is another service you could offer to others as well.

These are just a few examples of the many types of products that can be created with a laser. The possibilities are literally endless and can be adapted to any market and clientele. If you have a particular product in mind that you have never seen before, a laser machine is also a great tool to help bring that idea to life.

So now that you have some ideas, you probably have a rough plan on sizes and quantities. You can combine that with what we know as far as laser capabilities. You know your budget and things are starting to fall into place a bit. Before you purchase all the things, you might want to have a little reassurance that you are not wasting money. We need to do some market research and see if your ideas will actually turn a profit for you. There are several ways you can research the market demand for products. If you ask the internet you will get a bunch of answers like the following:

-Take surveys: Conduct surveys to get direct feedback from potential customers. You can use online survey tools or conduct in-person interviews to collect data. This can be very time consuming and tedious, but could help. Personally, I don't have the patience for this.

-Analyze search engine data: Use tools such as Google Trends and Keyword Planner to analyze search engine data and find out what people are searching for related to your product. (Side note: when you start selling, using these keywords in your product description and SEO on your website will bring in more traffic to your products.) This is incredibly effective and helpful.

-Analyze competition: Look at your competitors and

analyze their products, pricing, and marketing strategies to understand the demand for similar products. You can easily do this by checking out local boutiques and craft fairs. You can see the quality of their work as what they find to be good price points. Check out the facebook pages and other social media for these businesses and see what people are loving on their pages. If you go back a few times, you might notice which items seem to be selling the most. You could ask them but chances are they will know what you are doing and not want to give up all the information.

-Monitor industry trends: Keep up-to-date with industry trends and changes in consumer behavior to understand market demand and stay ahead of the competition. If you pay attention to what sites like Etsy are advertising most, as well as what people are sharing and pinning on pinterest, you will get a decent idea of the trends.

By using these methods, you can gather valuable information about your target market and their needs, which will help you make informed decisions about your product and marketing strategies.

Most likely you will find many of those ways too time consuming and not what you want to spend your valuable time doing. I am including them only to plant a seed for you as alternative ways to learn about the markets. I will guess you most likely will just start by making things that you like and seeing how that plays out. Pay attention to what people are buying. You will probably, like myself, be surprised from time to time when things that you never thought would sell are suddenly flying off the shelf. The opposite will also happen, when you make something that you think will be a huge seller and it just sits. These trends also change constantly so be ready to adjust and adapt. Try to pick products that can adapt also and be more versatile.

This process is never ending. You will need to think about it now and reevaluate continuously. Either mentally or on paper: Consider who is your target audience. Is the product aligned with your target audience's needs, preferences, and purchasing habits? Is there room for profitability? Calculate the cost of production, marketing, and fulfillment. Determine a price point that makes sense and generates profits. Are there already many similar products on the market? Is it a crowded and competitive industry? Analyze the competition and identify how you can differentiate your product from competitors. Does the product align with your brand identity? Does it compliment your existing product line or service offerings? Is the product a seasonal item or one that will sell year-round? Consider whether it's worth investing in a product that has a limited sales window. Is the product on-trend? Will it still be relevant and popular over time? It is also important to test new products before committing to them. Maybe just get a few to start out and see how well they sell before getting large quantities. Collect feedback from customers and test your product in different markets to understand its sales potential. This will help you make informed decisions and ensure that the products you sell align with your business goals and objectives.

Don't stress too much over this though. As long as you test first before over committing, if it fails, at least you learned something. There is a serious learning curve to beginning work with a laser. You will make mistakes and you will have other issues that you didn't foresee. Things can get bumped or moved, settings can be off, things can not be lined up correctly, or you can have hardware or software issues. Make sure you are ready for those things, especially early on. Take notes on your settings also, they will continue to come in very handy to save time and money in the future.

CHAPTER 4: MATERIALS AND SUPPLIES

To create great products, you'll need to have the right materials and supplies on hand. In this chapter, we'll explore different materials and supplies you may need, where to source them, and how to manage your inventory. There is no way that I could possibly guess all the materials and products that you will ever want. So of course, this is only a basic list and should help you with ideas to start looking and what to look for when purchasing.

When choosing a supplier to source your materials and blanks, be sure to consider the cost, quality of materials, shipping times and fees, and the variety of products offered. It's important to do thorough research on the materials you plan to use and finding a reliable and reputable supplier for your business. Ask questions about the chemicals used and research any safety concerns there might be when introducing this material to the heat of a laser. Also, read the reviews. You can learn so much about whether or not it will be a good fit for you based on other peoples experiences.

Many big-box craft stores carry a variety of materials that can be used for laser engraving and cutting, including wood, acrylic, and leather. These stores may also sell pre-cut plain and pre-finished blanks for specific projects. Added tip, Michael's craft store has a pro section online where you can purchase items at a bulk rate. These items are different from what is available in store and at much more appealing prices.

Online marketplaces like Amazon, Wish or Temu offer a wide variety of materials and blanks for laser engraving, including wood, acrylic, glass, and metal, as well as pre-cut and pre-finished blanks for specific projects. This is an excellent source of materials. Even if you find another source, using the materials that you find at low prices is a great way to practice your skill and do test runs with your laser to achieve your desired results. You will most likely find lower quality items from these types of places, that doesn't mean you can't make beautiful things with them and sell them for decent money. Over time, you may find that you want to increase your quality so that you are able to make more money while selling fewer things at higher prices.

There are many suppliers that specialize in materials for laser engraving and cutting, such as Johnson Plastics Plus, Trotec, and JDS Industries. That is just a few that are out there. Searching for specific items will help you to find suppliers that specialize in what you are looking for. These suppliers offer a range of materials including various types of acrylic, wood, leather and more. They also very often offer superior products to what you might find on Amazon and such. It is a bigger initial investment for your business but the quality will speak volumes and most likely create return customers. Some of these companies are also willing to send samples for you to test out before you commit to large quantity orders. This is definitely something you will want to take advantage of.

Depending on where you live, you may have access to local suppliers that carry materials for laser engraving. Look for suppliers of plastic sheets, acrylic, wood and leather in your area. Some local cabinet shops or things of that nature will often sell or give away scraps.

You may also find items at everyday stores like Walmart

and Target. They typically have decent craft items that can be customized. Always check for clearance sections as well and stock up when the prices are right.

When I first started, I went to thrift stores to search for materials to practice on. Occasionally, I would come across a jackpot. One time at Goodwill, I found a stock pile of bamboo cutting boards still in the plastic wrapper for a fraction of the price I would have paid for them anywhere else. You just never know where you might find things. As you continue on this journey, you will develop an eye for hunting deals and ideas. You will be amazed at the places you will discover things.

So let's just say you wanted to engrave tumblers for example. There are many styles, sizes, brands, and colors to choose from. There are also many extra features like straws, different lids and handles. Think of this example when I try to explain some of the material issues you may face.

When you are trying to source materials, you will want to think about how you will sell them. If you buy many styles from many brands with all sorts of variations, you will have to post about them all separately or people will not be able to accurately make a selection.

People have very different preferences. You do not need to appeal to everyone, the right people will find you. If you have too many options, you will only create more work for yourself and more confusion for your customers.

That being said, if you offer a very specific product, you might want to make sure you are able to source it from multiple locations. Occasionally, you will run into supply issues. You need to make sure you have purchasing options.

I honestly did not consider these things when I first started. Then I tried to make a website and had to post so many different items to show the options and variations and learned very quickly that the time and energy required to add all the details for things like that, especially when it's a brand new website, is not worth it at all. You will consume so many resources as far as posting and pictures and SEO and all those types of factors that you will surely become very frustrated with the whole selling process. At least for beginners, I highly recommend starting with a smaller amount of options. This way you can fine tune your processes all the way from production to selling and marketing to even shipping.

If you are only going to be doing in person selling, having all one off items is not such a big deal. What you might run into often with this is people wanting a different combination then what you have already created. For this, you will want to have a plan to allow them to custom order. You will need to consider things like how to get them the items after, if there will need to be an additional charge for custom designs, and most importantly get their contact information. If you just hand out a business card, more often than not, you will never hear from them again. If you get their info, you are at least able to follow up and try to make the sale. Try not to be too pushy, there will still be the people who won't return the call, text or email that you send out. That's ok, but without their information, you are left hoping they remember to call you back. I got a little off topic there but it is still a valuable point.

Going back to materials, you will also want to make sure you create a system that will work for you to control your inventory. This can be on paper or a spreadsheet or an app. Somehow, you need to know what you have. It is very helpful if you are able to access this information on the go. There will be times when you are out and about either just in normal life or at an event where someone will ask if you are able to do something for them. Knowing if you have the items will certainly help as far as telling them an estimated completion date. It will also help you know when you need to order more of certain materials in normal everyday business in the office. If you are like me, if you are not looking at it directly, it's very easy to forget exactly what you have. Integrating this system into your Point of Sale system can also help you to know when things are purchased to signal you to order more of something before you get too low on inventory. It is also a great reference to look back at trends. You can learn alot about which of your items are selling most. You can also see if the material costs are going up and you may need to adjust your prices accordingly.

Knowing what you have on hand can also help inspire new ideas or even let you know if there is something you may want to put on sale that has been sitting for a while. Occasionally you will need to cut your losses and sell things at a lower price point just to move them and then you will know that was probably not the best choice of product and learn from it.

When you are shopping for materials you will need to buy things that you will use more indirectly as well. Things like paint, stain, packaging, labels, ribbon, string, tape or other accessories. These are also things you may want to find that work well for you and you can stay consistent with. For example, you may want to make sure you can offer a few colors of stain consistently as options for custom orders. You also may want to achieve a certain look with your packaging. Also, having certain ribbons for bows and twine to hang signs with helps with limiting options. There are some things that you will find you go through a lot of, for me one of those things is tape. I often use it in my laser to hold items in place. I also use it on tumblers to mark out an area that I intend to engrave on. That way when I run the framing of the laser I know it will line up right. I also use it to block off different areas for painting or staining. My point to all of this is that these items, even though you don't consider them in the materials initially, very much still need to be sourced and tracked just like the main materials you are using. Without these items, you can't effectively do your job.

All of the things we talked about in this chapter also need to be factored into the cost of your items. You need to remember, as I mentioned before, to include material cost, tax, shipping and all other sub materials into the overall cost of making your products. It is easy to just see a wood blank at a store for $3 and say, well I can engrave it and sell it for $15. I will make $12 profit. Ok, but if you need to add a hanger to the back, stain it, poly it and stick a bow on it, you will not be making a profit at all on this item. That also doesn't account for your time, wear on your equipment, if you are using a POS (point of sale) system that charges a card use fee, and packaging if you have to ship the item. I know I am getting off topic again, I'm sorry but it will probably not be the last time. There are many factors that play a role in making a business profitable and they all tie together. It is a delicate balancing act trying to make it all work in harmony and it's easy to overlook things when focusing on something else.

CHAPTER 5: DESIGN AND PRODUCTION

Design and production are two of the most important elements in creating your products. In this chapter, we'll discuss design software, production techniques, and how to manage your workflow for maximum efficiency.

Since this book is intended for people just beginning, I will first give you a quick explanation of file types and how they work differently in a laser. There are definitely times when you will want one kind over another. Images can be saved in various file formats, each with its own characteristics and intended usage. Here are some common image file formats and their differences:

JPEG (Joint Photographic Experts Group): JPEG is a widely used and highly compressed file format. It is suitable for photographs and complex images with gradients or continuous tones. JPEG uses lossy compression, meaning some image quality may be lost to reduce file size. It supports millions of colors but does not support transparency.

PNG (Portable Network Graphics): PNG is a lossless file format that supports both indexed color and millions of colors. It is commonly used for computer-generated graphics, illustrations, and images that require transparency. PNG files do not lose quality when saved, making them suitable for detailed or text-heavy images. However, they tend to have larger file sizes compared to JPEG.

GIF (Graphics Interchange Format): GIF is a widely used file format for simple graphics, animations, and small file sizes. It uses lossless compression and supports transparency. GIFs are limited to a maximum of 256 colors, making them suitable for line art, logos, and simple animations. However, they are not ideal for complex or high-quality photographic images due to limited color support.

TIFF (Tagged Image File Format): TIFF is a flexible file format that supports lossless compression, making it suitable for high-quality images and professional printing. TIFF files can save images in both RGB and CMYK color spaces and support layers, transparency, and multiple image types such as grayscale and color. However, TIFF files tend to have larger file sizes compared to other formats.

BMP (Bitmap): BMP is a simple and commonly used file format for Windows-based computers. It uses uncompressed, lossless data, resulting in larger file sizes. BMP files support both monochrome and color images but do not offer advanced features like layers or transparency.

SVG (Scalable Vector Graphics): SVG is a vector-based file format that uses XML-based text format to describe 2D graphics. SVG files are resolution-independent, meaning they can be scaled up or down without loss of quality. They are ideal for logos, icons, and illustrations, and can be edited with vector graphics software.

RAW: RAW is a file format that contains unprocessed image data captured by digital cameras. It preserves the complete information captured by the camera's sensor, offering greater flexibility for post-processing. RAW files are typically larger and require specialized software to edit and convert to other formats.

These are just a few examples of common image file formats and their differences. Each format has its own strengths and intended use cases, so choosing the appropriate format depends on factors such as image content, quality requirements, transparency needs, and file size considerations.

I will give you a quick example of why the file types matter. If you wanted to cut out a layered shadow box, you would definitely want all the layers to be in SVG format. This will ensure a nice clean cut and scaling that will ensure your items line up perfectly. If you are wanting to engrave a photograph into wood, you will want that to be PNG to make sure that the grayscale of the image shows up nicely. You can work with JPEG as well but I would say that typically I almost exclusively use SVG or PNG. It might be just my own personal style but it is what I find to be most effective.

That being said, sometimes you like an image that isn't currently in the correct format to make it work for you. There are websites such as Free SVG Converter or ImagR that can help convert what you have currently into the format that will yield the correct results.

There are a variety of online resources where you can download images in SVG or PNG format for laser cutting and engraving. I will list a few and what I know about them. There are constantly new and better apps and websites being developed that do some of these things and for all I know, by the time this book is for sale the newest, best site will be out and so popular that you will be wondering why on earth I didn't include it. The truth is, never settle into any one of them so much so that you stop looking for more. The features and capabilities are advancing so quickly that doing that will only hold you back. Your competition will find them and the ease and efficiency that they will bring to the table could set them far ahead of you. Never limit yourself with the design aspect of this industry.

It is important to note that when using images that you did not design yourself, you need to make sure you are not breaking any trademark or copyright laws. If you are just making something for yourself to keep and not sell, it isn't a big deal to use a protected image. It doesn't break any copyright laws. However, when you are intending on selling items, you need to be careful and do it correctly. There are places where you can get free items with no copyright or public domain images. These are free to use without any repercussions. There are also sites to purchase individual items or unlimited use with a subscription. Make sure that the images you are downloading have a note attached saying that commercial usage is allowed or in some way indicating that you are receiving permission to replicate that image for your own financial gain when purchasing or downloading that particular image. Some websites and sellers may offer images only for personal use only, so be sure to read the license agreement before using the images.

Here are some popular options for finding premade images that you can download to use.

Freepik: Offers a wide range of vector images in SVG format that can be used for laser cutting and engraving. Many of these vector images are free to download and use, while others require a premium membership.

VectorStock: Offers a large selection of vector images in SVG format. These images can be purchased individually or through a subscription plan.

The Noun Project: Offers a large selection of icons and vector graphics in SVG format that can be used for laser cutting and engraving. Many of these images are available for free with attribution, or for a small fee for commercial use.

Shutterstock: Offers a large selection of vector images in SVG format for purchase. They offer various pricing plans for different levels of access.

Etsy: Is a great source for finding SVG and PNG images that are specifically designed for laser cutting and engraving. You can purchase premade designs or work with an artist to create custom designs.

Creative Fabrica: Offers a large selection of vector images in

SVG format and well as PNG and other formatted images. This site also has a large selection of fonts that can be downloaded and other training resources available. You can purchase items individually or on a subscription plan.

There are also sites that can help you to design your own images. These are just a few options available, and each platform has its strengths and weaknesses. It's recommended to explore these options, try them out, and find the one that suits your specific needs and preferences.

Adobe Illustrator is a professional-grade vector graphics editor that allows you to create and modify SVG files with a wide range of tools and features. It offers a free trial, as well as subscription-based plans.

Inkscape is a free and open-source vector graphics editor that supports SVG file format. It is a popular choice for designing and editing scalable vector graphics and offers a variety of tools and features comparable to commercial software.

Canva is a user-friendly online design tool that allows you to create custom graphics, including PNG files, with its drag-and-drop interface. While the free version offers a range of templates and design elements, Canva also has a paid subscription plan for additional features.

Vectr is a free vector graphics editor available both as a web-app and a downloadable software. It offers a straightforward interface with features for creating and editing SVG files collaboratively.

Gravit Designer is a free cross-platform vector graphics editor that can help you design both SVG and PNG files. It offers a range of tools, effects, and templates to create professional-level designs.

Vecteezy is an online platform that provides a wide array of customizable SVG graphics and resources. While it primarily offers pre-designed graphic elements, it also has a feature that allows some level of customization if you prefer to modify existing designs.

Procreate is an online platform that can help you draw images and download them to be used in multiple formats. This app is only for iphone and ipad. It does however also allow for different layers to be created which can be very helpful.

There also are certain design space apps that come with some particular lasers that offer limited design features to create images directly within the lasers software itself. These lists are in no way all inclusive and I am not trying to promote any of these more than others, it is simply a starting point for you to find ways and places to get the designs that you want and need.

You will eventually, probably sooner than later, decide that you want an external harddrive to hold all of the downloads. Not only will it help with space issues on your computer but it will also help you switch between devices much easier.

For a small business, it is important to focus on production techniques that maximize efficiency, optimize resources, and maintain quality. Some of these will not be relevant to your business until it grows. However, they will certainly still help you even if your business is only you making things. These practices are things that even large corporations use to be as efficient as possible. Efficiency is something that should definitely be used as a small business as well where the phrase time is money is even more relevant.

I wish I could tell you that I just got all this information about efficiency from the internet, but that is not the case. Much of this comes from those jobs I mentioned, in the intro of this book, that I had previously and did not like. As much as I did not enjoy the work I was doing, it did teach me so much about production and efficiency. For that, I am very grateful. That is how I know that these things work and why they are so important. Some people who have helped me, did not come from the same background and I can see that they take on tasks differently than I would. I try to show them the why's and how's to improve and even if they are not excited for the changes, the difference in the outcomes speaks for itself.

Here is a list of some important production techniques:

Lean Manufacturing: Lean manufacturing focuses on minimizing waste and maximizing productivity by identifying and eliminating unnecessary steps, processes, or resources. It involves streamlining workflows, reducing inventory, and improving overall efficiency. Implementing lean principles can help small businesses reduce costs, improve lead times, and increase customer satisfaction.

Just-In-Time (JIT) Production: JIT production aims to minimize inventory costs by producing goods or services only when they are needed. This technique helps prevent excess inventory and reduces storage costs. By closely monitoring demand and adjusting production accordingly, small businesses can optimize their resources and respond quickly to changing market demands.

Quality Control: Maintaining consistent quality is crucial for small businesses to build a strong reputation and satisfy customer expectations. Implementing quality control measures helps identify and rectify any production errors or defects before the product reaches the customer. Quality control techniques may involve regular inspections, product testing, and feedback loops to continuously improve processes and output.

Automation and Technology: Embracing automation and technology can significantly enhance production efficiency for small businesses. Implementing computerized systems, machinery, or software can reduce human error, speed up processes, and increase productivity. Small businesses can consider adopting tools for inventory management, production scheduling, or data analysis to streamline operations and make more informed decisions. Even though it seems like it is not relevant to a small business it is. We have touched on many things tied to this already but even just things like making jigs to be able to line up items consistently every time would fall into this category.

Cross-Training and Flexibility: Small businesses often face resource constraints and fluctuations in demand. Cross-training employees across different tasks or functions can provide flexibility in production operations. This approach helps ensure that operations can continue smoothly even if certain employees are absent, and it allows for better utilization of available resources.

Continuous Improvement: Adopting a culture of continuous improvement is essential for small businesses to stay competitive and adapt to changing market conditions. This involves regularly evaluating processes, seeking feedback from customers and employees, and implementing changes to optimize efficiency and quality. Techniques like Kaizen, Six Sigma, or Total Quality Management (TQM) can help identify areas for improvement and drive innovation.

Supplier Management: Efficient supply chain management is crucial for small businesses to ensure a steady supply of raw materials or components. Building strong relationships with reliable suppliers can help secure favorable terms, timely deliveries, and optimal pricing. Effective supplier management includes monitoring supplier performance, maintaining open communication, and exploring opportunities for collaboration.

By implementing these production techniques, small businesses can enhance their efficiency, reduce costs, improve product quality, and remain competitive in the market. It is important to regularly assess and adapt these techniques to meet the specific needs and challenges of the business. I did not go into full detail on each of these concepts but if any of them sound interesting there are many places to learn more about each technique online.

When you are a small business, especially if you are the only employee, it is critical to get as much done in as little time as possible. Often it helps to start by looking at your to-do list and determining which things are going to take multiple steps to complete. You should also note if there are many things that will require the same tool, in our case, that would probably be the laser itself. Some of what you will do will require other equipment as well, such as the rotary attachment, Even things like changing the setup of the laser take time. You will want to plan ahead to minimize this as much as possible. You will also want to think about products that will take longer in the laser and make sure that there are other things that you can be doing simultaneously that will help to complete other items or tasks while you wait.

Managing workflow efficiently will maximize productivity and optimize resources. Start each day by identifying and prioritizing the most important tasks. Use techniques like the Eisenhower Matrix or ABC analysis to categorize tasks based on urgency and importance. Focus on completing high-priority tasks first to ensure they are not neglected.

Break down complex tasks into smaller, manageable sub-tasks. This helps to avoid overwhelm and allows you to track progress more effectively. Use project management tools or to-do lists to organize and track these smaller tasks.

Set deadlines for tasks based on their priority and complexity. Ensure the deadlines are achievable, considering the available resources and other commitments. Building in buffer time for unexpected delays or interruptions can help prevent unnecessary stress. If you finish earlier, then great.

Identify tasks that can be delegated to team members or outsourced to external parties. Delegating tasks not only reduces your workload but also helps in building trust and empowering your team. Be clear about expectations, provide necessary resources, and regularly communicate to ensure smooth collaboration. Communication is key as well as not allowing yourself to be overloaded unnecessarily. You might even be surprised about what others can do that you didn't even know was possible.

Effective communication plays a crucial role in workflow management. Use collaboration and communication tools, such as project management software or team messaging apps, to streamline communication and ensure everyone is on the same page. Clearly define roles, expectations, and deadlines while encouraging open communication and feedback. Side note to this, my team even all share images related to the company to one google photos album so we can all access things as needed.

Identify repetitive or time-consuming tasks that can be automated using technology or software. This can include tasks like data entry, report generation, or email notifications. Automating such tasks not only saves time but also reduces the risk of human error. There are even apps that can automate your posts to social media and other advertising.

Multitasking can often lead to reduced productivity and quality of work. Instead, focus on one task at a time to ensure better concentration and efficiency. Complete or reach a milestone in one task before moving on to the next. I know I already said to try to do things to fill your time while other things are happening, that is a little different than multitasking. When I say multitasking I am referring to doing multiple things that take your primary focus all at the same time. If you are sanding something and then staining it while your laser is engraving the next piece and you are just nearby for safety purposes, that is not the same as trying to work with a customer on the details of a sale while packaging and pricing products. In the second scenario, you are bound to make mistakes on both ends.

Identify and minimize distractions that hamper your

workflow. This can include turning off notifications, setting specific times for checking emails or messages, or creating a dedicated workspace free from distractions. Use productivity techniques like the Pomodoro Technique, where you work in focused sprints followed by short breaks, to maintain focus.

Continuously assess your workflow to identify any bottlenecks or areas for improvement. Seek feedback from team members and iterate on your processes. Implementing process improvement methodologies like Lean or Six Sigma can help streamline workflows and drive efficiency.

Taking breaks and practicing self-care is crucial for maintaining productivity and overall well-being. Schedule regular breaks, engage in physical activity, and ensure you get enough sleep and nourishment. By taking care of yourself, you can maintain focus and energy throughout the workday.

Owning a business, especially in the early stages, can be exhausting. You can easily burn yourself out to the point of throwing in the towel if you don't remember to take time for yourself. I can also guarantee you that at some point in the process, you will be neck deep in making things happen and at least one other person in your life will come to you and say you need to remember to take care of yourself. It is so easy to get so deep into all that goes along with a startup that you will neglect yourself. So easy in fact, that I know it will happen to each and every one of us many times over. Try to remind yourself before someone else has to.

Remember that managing workflow efficiently is an ongoing process. Regularly review and adapt your strategies based on the needs of your work and the feedback you receive. In time, this will become second nature. The more of these strategies that you implement, the more of a difference you will see.

CHAPTER 6: PRICING YOUR PRODUCTS

Setting the right price for your products can make or break your business. It is also one the absolute hardest things for me to do personally. I look at things and think about the similar item I saw over at Hobby Lobby and what that price was. I also think about what I would pay for something, and well, I am kinda cheap. I also see every little flaw in something and am my own worst critic. I am going to guess that I am not the only one. Here is what I have learned about this. People love to pay more for handmade, one off or custom items. They enjoy the craftsmanship and hard work that goes into them. They also love the customization and story that comes with a piece that did not come off the shelf of a chain store. They also seem to think that the "flaws" that we see in our own work are not flaws at all and in fact just add character to the item. That being said, many of my customers told me that I am undervaluing my work. My team tried telling me that I should not be in charge of setting prices. All of these people were absolutely correct. I was undervaluing my work. I was also making very little profit because of this, so much so that it was taking far longer than it should for me to be able to do what I love full time. Please, learn from my mistake and price your items appropriately. Trying to be the cheapest will hurt you. Some people will even think your quality is lesser than your competition if your prices are lower.

In this chapter, we'll explore different pricing strategies, how to calculate your costs, and how to determine your profit margins.

Deciding on a good price for products you have made can be challenging. There are a few key factors to consider, for starters, cost of materials. You should determine the cost of the materials used to create the product. This includes everything from the raw materials to any tools or equipment used in the process. Wear and tear on equipment and the electricity to run them cost you money over time and therefore need to be factored in as well.

You should also consider the amount of time and effort it took to create the product. This includes the time spent researching, designing, and manufacturing the product.

Look at what similar products are selling for in the market. Based on the competition, you can determine whether your product is under or overpriced.

Consider your target market and how much they are willing to pay for your product. For example, luxury items may warrant a higher price point because the target market is willing to pay more for the perceived value.

Determine how much you want to make in profit. This will vary depending on your business goals and how much you need to cover your costs. Try to set your prices to make as much profit as you can. Keep in mind setting your prices too high will scare off customers.

Once you have considered these factors, you can set a price that covers your costs and provides a reasonable profit margin while still being competitive in the market. Remember to regularly review your pricing to ensure it remains competitive and profitable. Material costs are ever changing as well. You need to increase accordingly.

Setting the right price for your products is crucial for the success and profitability of your business. There are several different strategies that people take to do this. It all depends on what you think is the right way to go about it. I will list a few different ways.

Cost-Based Pricing: This strategy involves setting prices based on the production costs of the product, including raw materials, labor, and overhead expenses. It typically involves adding a markup or profit margin to the total cost to determine the selling price. Cost-based pricing provides a straightforward approach but may not consider market demand or competition.

Market-Based Pricing: Market-based pricing involves setting prices based on market conditions, demand levels, and competition. It involves researching and analyzing the prices of similar products in the market and positioning your product accordingly. This strategy can help align your prices with customer expectations and market dynamics.

Value-Based Pricing: Value-based pricing focuses on setting prices based on the perceived value or benefits that the product offers to customers. It emphasizes the value proposition of the product and pricing it accordingly. This approach can be effective when your product offers unique features, superior quality, or a differentiated value proposition compared to competitors.

Competitive Pricing: This strategy involves setting prices in line with or slightly lower than competitors' prices. It aims to attract customers by offering a competitive price while maintaining a comparable level of product quality. Competitive pricing is often used in highly competitive markets where price plays a significant role in customer decision-making.

Psychological Pricing: Psychological pricing leverages consumer psychology and perception to influence purchasing behavior. It involves setting prices that have a psychological impact on customers, such as using charm prices ($9.99 instead of $10) or bundle pricing (offering discounts when purchasing multiple items together). Psychological pricing can create the perception of value or affordability for customers.

Premium Pricing: Premium pricing is a strategy of setting higher prices to position your product as a high-quality or luxury offering. This strategy is suitable for products that have unique features, superior quality, or a strong brand reputation. Premium pricing aims to communicate value and exclusivity to customers while capturing a niche segment willing to pay a higher price.

Penetration Pricing: Penetration pricing involves setting low initial prices to quickly gain market share and attract customers. This strategy is often used when entering a new market or introducing a new product. The goal is to encourage trial and adoption by offering a competitive price advantage. Once a customer base is established, prices can be gradually increased.

Price Skimming: Price skimming involves setting high prices initially, targeting early adopters or customers who are willing to pay a premium for a new or innovative product. Over time, prices are gradually decreased to attract more price-sensitive customers. Price skimming is often used for products with limited competition or a unique value proposition.

It's important to consider multiple factors, such as production costs, competitive landscape, customer perception, and market dynamics, when selecting a pricing strategy. It may also be necessary to adjust pricing over time based on changes in costs, demand, or positioning. Regularly review and analyze your pricing strategy to ensure it aligns with your business goals and maximizes profitability. This is something that only you will be able to decide what works best and feels right to you.

I know we have touched on this many times but calculating the price for your products involves considering several factors. Here's a step-by-step approach to help you determine the best price:

Determine your costs: Start by calculating all the costs associated with producing your product. This includes the cost of raw materials, manufacturing or production costs, labor costs, shipping and logistics expenses, overhead costs, and any other relevant expenses. Make sure to allocate your costs accurately and include both direct and indirect costs.

Research the market: Study your target market and analyze similar products or services. Look for pricing trends, competitor prices, and customer preferences. This research will give you valuable insights into the price range and competitive landscape for your product.

Define your value proposition: Determine the unique value and benefits your product offers to customers. Consider factors such as quality, features, brand reputation, customer service, and any other differentiating factors. This will help you position your product and set an appropriate price based on its perceived value.

Assess customer willingness to pay: Understand the price sensitivity of your target customers. This can be done through market research, customer surveys, or analyzing customer behavior and feedback. Assess how much customers are willing to pay for your product based on their perceived value and their financial capability.

Consider pricing strategies: Evaluate the different pricing strategies discussed earlier (cost-based, market-based, value-based, etc.) and choose the one that aligns best with your business goals. Adopting a specific pricing strategy will guide your decision-making process.

Set profit margins: Determine the profit margin you want to achieve for each product sold. Profit margin is the difference between the selling price and the total cost per unit. It helps ensure you generate enough revenue to cover costs and make a profit.

Test and adjust: Once you have determined a price, consider testing it in the market. Monitor customer response, sales volumes, and profitability. If the price is not generating the desired results, be open to adjusting it based on market feedback and business objectives.

Remember, pricing is not a one-time decision. It requires ongoing monitoring and adjustment to adapt to market changes, competitive dynamics, and customer preferences. Regularly review your pricing strategy to ensure it remains competitive, profitable, and aligned with your business goals.

Determining your profit margins involves calculating the difference between your selling price and the total cost per unit. Here's how you can determine your profit margins:

Add up all the costs associated with producing or acquiring a single unit of your product. This includes direct costs (such as materials, labor, and manufacturing) as well as indirect costs (such as overhead expenses, marketing, and administrative costs). Be sure to consider all relevant costs to get an accurate total cost per unit.

Consider various factors when setting your selling price, such as market demand, competition, customer perception, and your business goals. Your selling price should be both competitive and able to cover your costs while generating a profit. For example, if your total cost per unit is $10 and you want to achieve a 20% profit margin, your selling price should be $12 ($10 + $2 profit).

To determine your profit margin percentage, divide your profit (selling price minus total cost per unit) by the selling price, and multiply it by 100. For example, if your selling price is $12 and your total cost per unit is $10, your profit per unit is $2. Using the formula (profit\/selling price) * 100, your profit margin would be 16.67% ($2\/$12 * 100).

Analyze and adjust: Regularly analyze your profit margins to ensure they align with your business objectives and industry standards. If your profit margins are low, you may need to revisit your pricing, cost structure, or overall business strategy. Adjusting your costs, improving efficiency, or exploring opportunities for economies of scale can help increase profit margins.

It's important to note that profit margin percentages can vary across industries and business models. It's crucial to consider your specific industry dynamics and competitive landscape when determining the appropriate profit margins for your business. Regularly monitor your profit margins and make necessary adjustments to maintain profitability and sustainability.

CHAPTER 8: SELLING AT CRAFT FAIRS AND BOUTIQUES

Craft fairs and boutiques can be a great way to get your products in front of potential customers. In this chapter, we'll discuss how to find the right events, how to prepare for them, and how to make the most of your time and investment.

Selling at craft fairs can be a fantastic way to promote your products, connect with potential customers, and make sales. However, they do have some pros and cons to consider.

Starting with some of the pros, first the exposure. Craft fairs can be a great way to get exposure for your products and brand. You'll be in front of a large, diverse group of potential customers who are specifically interested in crafts and handmade goods. Often this will lead to custom orders and invitations to other events. You can hand out lots of business cards this way as well to drive customers to your social media and/or website.

Another great benefit to attending events is that you can network with other vendors and crafters. This can lead to possible partnership opportunities, collaboration options or even learning some new techniques from other vendors as well. Oftentimes they will help you to find more and better future events. You may even find people you can point you in the right direction to get items to better your display or signage.

An obvious benefit is that you can directly sell your

products to customers, which can be more efficient than relying on online sales. It also cuts down on shipping cost and possibly the credit card processing fees if they pay in cash.

Face-to-face interaction with customers can give you valuable feedback about your products. I have mentioned it before but you really can learn so much about what is working and what you can improve by making observations of the customers interests.

You can also showcase your branding and marketing materials to potential customers and create brand recognition in your local community. If you have a nice aesthetically pleasing display and packaging for items that showcases what you stand for and the vibe of your company, it draws in the people that you are targeting. I also tend to give away small items with a purchase that have my company name on them. People might lose a business card long before they will lose a small free gift.

Now to get into the cons. There may be costs such as booth fees, travel expenses, and time spent setting up and taking down your booth. At first you might think you want to find the cheapest booth fees that you can, however, you often get what you pay for. Event coordinators usually have a pretty good idea of the amount of traffic the event can expect. They also charge more so they can advertise it better. The cheaper events won't have the budget to advertise to large crowds.

Typically you can expect to devote your entire day to an event. Even if the craft fair is only open to the public for 6 hours. You will need to load up, travel there, unload, set up, attend the event, tear down, travel home, evaluate your day. You will most likely need help with all or some of these steps as well.

Craft fairs can be competitive and crowded, with many other vendors selling similar products. Typically coordinators will have you fill out a questionnaire detailing the items you will be selling. They may even ask for pictures. These pictures serve

2 purposes. First to make sure your items are not the same as any other registered sellers. You won't want that and neither will they. Second, they may use them to post on social media for advertising the event. Keep that in mind when submitting pictures.

Depending on the location of the craft fair, you may be exposed to outdoor elements such as heat, rain, or wind. You will want to dress accordingly and bring all possible items you will need to combat the elements. Once you are there you will most likely not have to send for other items and most events require you to remain set up until closing time. You will also want to make sure that your tables and canopies are weighed down. Not only can things blowing away damage your inventory but it can also wreck your fellow vendors' items. The cost of that damage would fall on you.

The duration of the fair can be short, leaving limited time to make sales. Some craft fairs only last a few hours. You may even notice that it took longer to get there, set up, tear down and get home than the amount of time for actual sales.

Sales can be inconsistent due to the unpredictable nature of the event. Time of year, weather, holidays, other community events and many other factors play a role in the attendance. Depending on who is there that day and if people are just looking or actually spending money will cause your overall sales to vary wildly.

Overall, selling at craft fairs can be a rewarding and profitable experience, but it's important to weigh the pros and cons and determine if it's the right choice for your business.

There are several other places where you can sell things that you make, such as consignment shops. They allow you to place your products for sale in their store. The shop will take a percentage of the sale price as a commission. This option is good for people who don't have their own sales space but still want to sell their products in person. This also means that you can just restock as needed as opposed to hauling things around to craft fairs.

Farmer's markets are also great places to sell handmade products, especially if they're related to food items, such as jams, bread, baked goods or any other homemade food items. Some farmers markets have rules that they need to be food items. Others will allow you to sell most anything.

Pop-up shops are temporary retail spaces that allow you to showcase and sell your products in a physical location. You can use pop-up shops to test new products or build brand awareness.

Local boutiques are small stores that may intentionally focus on locally made and unique products. You can approach the stores directly to see if they're interested in selling your products. You might be able to work out a deal with them to sell items with their logo and they resell the items. Alternatively, some stores will set up a corner just for your items if they think it is a good addition to their store and they will handle the sales for you for a fee. Some boutiques mix everyone's items together to create a more unified overall store appearance.

Trade shows can be a great way to connect with retailers and other buyers in your industry. These events allow you to showcase your products to a large and diversified audience.

You can sell your products at community events such as art fairs, concerts, and festivals. These events typically draw large crowds and give you a chance to promote your products to people who might not otherwise see them.

Keep in mind that selling in person can require a lot more time and effort than selling online. You will need to consider factors such as transportation, storing, display, and staffing. However, the benefits of in-person selling can be significant, and you may generate more exposure and sales through these outlets.

When you are looking to find events to attend, go back to

those facebook groups we talked about before. There are many groups dedicated to just this. Typically there are several groups for each state, or region within a state. Within there you will see several posts about events. Don't be afraid to ask questions. You might want to try out an event with a new coordinator before committing to multiple events with them. You might find that there are some organizations that you love and some that you never want to deal with again.

Also, because people know that crafters pay fees to attend events it opens up the world of scammers into our industry. This means that you want to do your due diligence to make sure that you are contacting genuine organizations and the correct contact person to send your money to beforehand. I wish it was not the case but there are many people out there that will try to trick you out of money.

Other things that you will want to plan for is your display. How your items can best be showcased will make or break sales. Some people will walk right by your booth without even stepping one foot in or giving you a second look if it doesn't appear inviting. You will want to give this lots of thought and careful consideration. Also, as with everything else, pay attention to what is or is not working and change things accordingly for the next time. I have never set up the same way twice.

You will want to make sure your items are either all individually priced or that you have signs indicating the prices. Most people will not ask you about prices.

Also, think about how you want to accept payment. We all love getting paid in cash but most people don't care much if any with them. You would think that going to these events people will pull out cash ahead of time, however, if they are almost out of money and you don't take cards, you will inevitably miss out on sales. There are so many POS systems to choose from. Deciding early can be a great idea because many of the features that go along with that trickle down to several other aspects of your business.

Many have features that can be incredibly helpful that you have not even considered yet. Others may have lots of hidden fees or very bad reviews from dissatisfied customers. You will want to take your time looking into several options before making your choice.

You will also want to have a good idea of your inventory that you are bringing with you to events. The same goes for selling in boutiques or consignment stores also. This can be helpful in a couple ways. First you can track what is selling so you can better watch for trends. But also, this will help you notice stolen or lost items.

CHAPTER 9: MANAGING YOUR FINANCES

With any small business, it's important to keep track of your finances. In this chapter, we'll discuss how to manage your accounting, taxes, and cash flow.

Set up a separate business bank account: A separate bank account helps you keep your personal finances separate from your business finances. It also makes it easy to track your business transactions and reconcile your books. Depending on your business structure, this might not even be optional but rather necessary.

Keep track of all your income and expenses and maintain accurate records. This will help you stay on top of your cash flow, prepare for taxes, and make informed business decisions. You will also want to save receipts. You don't have to keep boxes or bags of old receipts anymore with the help of apps that will take pictures of them and track expenses for you.

Accounting software like Quickbooks, Xero, or FreshBooks can help you streamline your accounting processes, generate financial reports, and track your cash flow. Most of these also have ways to send things right over to your tax specialist which will save you so much time in tax season.

If accounting is not your specialty, consider hiring an accountant or bookkeeper to manage your finances. They can handle tasks such as bookkeeping, payroll, and tax preparation, giving you more time to focus on growing your business. Some might also be able to advise you on financial planning to help grow your business quicker.

Make sure to keep up with your tax obligations, including sales tax, income tax, payroll tax, and any other applicable taxes. Set aside money each month to cover your tax liabilities and consult a tax professional if you have any questions. You will want to find out if you need to file annually or quarterly. This will most likely depend on business structure and total sales. Typically there is a threshold that if you make more than $X/ month you will have to switch to quarterly filings. You can look it up online or call your department of revenue to ask them. Having to pay in more than you expect at the end of the year can be crippling. It is better to plan ahead and set money aside often to be used when it is time.

Forecasts will help you plan your expenses, predict revenue, and estimate the amount of cash needed to run your business successfully. This can help you decide when to make purchases and when to delay expenses.

While bookkeeping and taxes are crucial components of financial management for small businesses, there are other key considerations for maintaining healthy finances and cash flow. You will want to keep in mind budgeting. Develop a comprehensive budget that outlines your expected income and expenses. This allows you to plan and allocate your financial resources effectively. Regularly review and adjust your budget as needed to ensure you stay on track.

Monitor and manage your cash flow closely to ensure you have enough liquidity to cover your expenses. Maintain a cash flow forecast that estimates your future cash inflows and outflows. Utilize strategies such as optimizing payment terms, implementing effective credit and collection policies, and managing inventory levels to improve cash flow.

Develop strong relationships with your vendors and suppliers. Negotiate favorable payment terms, discounts, or rebates if possible. Timely payments and effective communication can help maintain positive relationships and potentially access better pricing or payment options.

If your business extends credit to customers, establish clear credit policies and procedures. Conduct credit checks on new customers, establish credit limits and payment terms, and regularly monitor customer payment behavior. Promptly follow up on overdue payments and consider utilizing collection agencies or legal action if necessary.

Consistently monitor and control your expenses to improve profitability. Review your overhead costs regularly and identify areas where you can reduce expenses without sacrificing quality. Negotiate with suppliers, explore cost-saving technologies, and streamline your operations to increase efficiency and reduce costs.

Regularly analyze and interpret your financial statements, such as profit and loss statements, balance sheets, and cash flow statements. Use financial ratios and key performance indicators (KPIs) to assess your business's financial health and performance. Identify trends, strengths, and weaknesses, and make data-driven decisions to improve your financial outcomes.

Establish and maintain an emergency fund to handle unforeseen expenses or periods of reduced revenue. This buffer provides a financial safety net and helps you avoid relying on short-term loans or incurring debt during challenging times.

If your business has debt, develop a repayment plan to manage it effectively. Regularly review your interest rates, loan terms, and payment schedules to identify opportunities for refinancing or consolidating debt. Prioritize paying off high-interest debt first to reduce overall interest costs.

Consider seeking professional advice from accountants, financial advisors, or business consultants. They can offer guidance on financial matters, tax planning, business strategies, and investment opportunities. Their expertise can help you make informed decisions and optimize your financial management.

CHAPTER 7: MARKETING AND BRANDING

Once you have your products and pricing in place, it's time to start getting the word out. In this chapter, we'll explore different marketing techniques, how to define your brand, and how to create a strong online presence.

There are many strategies for marketing products online, but here are some of the most effective ones:

Search Engine Optimization (SEO): SEO involves optimizing your website and product pages to help them rank higher on search engines such as Google. By using relevant keywords in your product descriptions and titles, you can attract more organic traffic to your website.

Social Media Marketing: Social media platforms are a great way to connect with potential customers and promote your products. You can use platforms

like Facebook, Instagram, and Twitter to build brand awareness, run targeted ads, and engage with your audience.

Email Marketing: Email marketing is another effective way to reach potential customers and build a relationship with them. You can use email to promote sales, new products, or exclusive offers and discounts.

Content Marketing: Creating valuable content such as blog

posts, tutorials, and videos can attract potential customers to your website and help establish your brand as an authority in your niche.

Influencer Marketing: Partnering with social media influencers can help you reach a wider audience and build trust in your brand.

Pay-Per-Click (PPC) Advertising: PPC marketing involves placing ads on search engines or social media platforms and paying for each time someone clicks on your ad. This can be a highly targeted and effective way to drive traffic to your website.

Ultimately, the best marketing strategy for your business will depend on your budget, target audience, and overall business goals. By implementing multiple strategies and continually monitoring the results, you can find the approach that works best for you.

Defining your brand is critical to creating a strong and recognizable identity that sets you apart from competitors. Start by gaining a deep understanding of your target audience's needs, desires, and preferences. Conduct market research, analyze customer data, and create buyer personas to identify your core audience segments.

This understanding will guide your brand development and messaging. This can be based off of extensive research if you want or it can be based off of observations you make in your own community. Since I have no idea what the scale of your business will be, I am just giving options.

Define the purpose and values that your brand stands for. Ask yourself why your brand exists and what it aims to achieve. Establish core values that resonate with your target audience and align with your products or services. Articulate your brand's mission and vision to serve as a guiding compass. Writing this down can help you focus.

Determine what sets your brand apart from competitors. Identify your unique selling points, key differentiators, or value propositions that make your brand and offerings unique. Highlight these strengths to shape your brand positioning in the market.

Define the personality traits, tone of voice, and style that reflect your brand. Consider if your brand is playful and humorous, professional and authoritative, or caring and empathetic. This personality should consistently permeate all aspects of your brand communication.

Choose a brand name that reflects your brand's personality, values, and positioning. Ensure it is easy to pronounce, spell, and remember. Develop a visually appealing logo, color palette, typography, and overall visual identity that align with your brand's essence and appeal to your target audience.

Craft clear and concise brand messaging that communicates your value proposition, key benefits, and unique attributes to your target audience. Consistently use this messaging across all communication channels, including your website, social media profiles, advertising, and customer interactions.

Consistency is vital in creating a strong brand identity. Ensure that all brand elements, including logos, colors, fonts, visuals, and tone of voice, are consistently used across all touchpoints and marketing materials. This consistency helps customers recognize and connect with your brand.

Your brand's reputation is built based on delivering what you promise. Consistently provide a high-quality product or service, excellent customer service, and a positive brand experience. Delighting customers and exceeding their expectations will solidify your brand reputation and generate loyalty.

Regularly monitor how your brand is perceived by customers and gather feedback to assess if it aligns with your brand identity. Make adjustments as needed to stay relevant, meet evolving customer expectations, and stay ahead of the competition.

Remember, building a brand takes time and consistency. It requires ongoing effort to nurture and maintain your brand's identity across all touchpoints and interactions. Stay true to your brand values and adapt as needed to create a strong and impactful brand that resonates with your target audience.

Creating a strong online presence for your company and products is crucial in today's digital landscape. Your website and social media platforms serve as the online face of your company. Ensure it is professionally designed, visually appealing, and user-friendly. Create relevant and engaging content that showcases your products, services, and brand. Optimize your website for search engines (SEO) to improve visibility and attract organic traffic.

Another very important aspect to all online traffic whether it be a website or social media is the pictures. Taking good product pictures is essential for effectively showcasing your products and attracting customers.

Good lighting is crucial for capturing clear and well-lit product images. Natural light is often best, so consider taking photos near a window during daylight hours. Alternatively, use soft, diffused artificial lighting setups to avoid harsh shadows or glares.

Choose a clean and clutter-free background that doesn't distract from the product. A solid color or a simple backdrop can work well. Ensure the background complements and enhances the product's aesthetics. Additionally, consider using props or contextual settings that help customers envision how the product can be used or its scale.

Compose your shots thoughtfully to highlight and emphasize the key features and details of the product. Use the rule of thirds or other composition techniques to create visually appealing and balanced images. Experiment with angles, close-ups, and different perspectives to showcase different aspects of the product.

Properly position and arrange the product in the frame to showcase its most important features. Highlight unique selling points and demonstrate its functionality, if applicable. Capture multiple angles and viewpoints to provide a comprehensive view of the product.

Ensure your product is in sharp focus, especially on the key focal points. Use a tripod or stabilize your camera to avoid camera shake and maintain sharpness. If necessary, use manual focus or focus stacking techniques to capture sharp details across the entire product.

Maintain a consistent style and branding across all your product images. Use a similar background, lighting, and composition to create a cohesive look. Consistency helps customers recognize and identify your brand and products.

Post-processing can enhance the quality and appeal of your product images. Use photo editing software to adjust brightness, contrast, color balance, and cropping. However, be mindful of not over editing or misrepresenting the product's actual appearance.

Provide a variety of images that show different angles, details, and uses of the product. This allows customers to get a complete understanding of the product's features and helps them make informed purchasing decisions.

Use a high-resolution camera or smartphone to capture detailed and clear images. However, ensure that the final images are optimized for the web to reduce file size and improve loading speed without compromising image quality.

Continuously test and improve your product photography. Analyze how your images perform in terms of engagement, conversions, and customer feedback. Make necessary adjustments to your approach based on data and customer preferences.

Remember, high-quality product images can significantly impact customers' perception and purchase decisions. Invest time and effort into capturing visually appealing and informative product photos to create a positive impression and increase your chances of success.

Now, back to posting those pictures and creating that presence. Identify the social media platforms that align with your target audience and engage with them effectively. Create business profiles on platforms such as Facebook, Instagram, Twitter, LinkedIn, or YouTube and regularly post engaging and valuable content. Be responsive to customer comments and inquiries to foster positive relationships.

Develop a content strategy that revolves around creating and sharing valuable, relevant, and engaging content with your target audience. Publish blog posts, articles, videos, or infographics that address their pain points, provide insights, or offer solutions. Optimize content for search engines and share it on social media to drive traffic and establish your authority in your industry.

Understand and implement SEO best practices to improve your website's visibility in search engine rankings. Research and incorporate relevant keywords, create quality backlinks, optimize page titles and meta descriptions, and ensure your website is fast, mobile-friendly, and provides a seamless user experience. If this sort of thing is not something you are good at, there are many people you can find online that will help you. It is easy to hire out much of the online side of things or even use AI.

Collaborate with influencers or industry experts who have a strong online presence and a relevant audience. Partner with them to promote your products or services through sponsored content, reviews, or endorsements. This can help you reach a wider audience and build credibility and trust.

Build an email list and engage with your subscribers through regular newsletters, product updates, exclusive offers, or personalized content. Use email automation tools to segment your audience and deliver targeted messages that resonate with their interests and needs.

Positive reviews and testimonials from satisfied customers can significantly impact your online reputation and credibility. Encourage customers to leave reviews on platforms such as Google, Yelp, or industry-specific review websites. Display these testimonials on your website or social media to showcase your brand's value.

Actively participate in relevant online communities, forums, or industry-specific groups. Offer valuable insights, answer questions, and establish yourself as an authority in your field. This can attract attention, build relationships, and drive traffic to your website.

Regularly track and analyze key metrics such as website traffic, social media engagement, conversion rates, and customer feedback. Use analytics tools to gain insights about your audience, identify trends, and make data-driven decisions to optimize your online presence and marketing efforts. You can easily get a Meta business suite that will show you this information about your facebook and Instagram business pages.

By implementing these strategies and techniques, you can create a strong and impactful online presence for your company and products, attracting and engaging with your target audience effectively. This may not be something that you wanted to be such a big part of your business, but it is very effective and often free advertisement.

CHAPTER 10: GROWING YOUR BUSINESS

As your business grows, you'll need to adapt and adjust your strategies for continued success. In this chapter, we'll discuss how to scale your business, add new products, and explore new markets.

Before exploring new markets, you need to understand your target audience. Conduct market research to identify consumer needs, preferences, and habits. Use this information to develop products and marketing strategies that appeal to your target audience.

Look for opportunities to add new products or services that complement your existing offerings. This can help you attract new customers and increase revenue.

Develop a strategic plan that outlines your goals, priorities, and resources. Identify potential risks, challenges, and opportunities. Develop action plans to mitigate risks and capitalize on opportunities.

Scaling your business often requires additional funds. Explore different funding options, including loans, grants, investments, and crowdfunding.

Use technology to streamline your business operations, enhance customer experience, and improve productivity. This can include adding an e-commerce store, introducing automation and AI, or implementing a CRM system.

Network with other entrepreneurs and industry leaders, attend trade shows, and participate in business communities. Collaborate on projects and partnerships to expand your reach and increase brand visibility.

Seek advice and feedback from mentors, advisors, and customers. Get feedback on your products, services, and marketing strategies. Use this feedback to make necessary adjustments and improvements.

By following these tips, you can scale your business, add new products, and explore new markets successfully. Remember to stay agile, be proactive, and monitor your progress regularly.

CHAPTER 11: MAKING SENSE OF ALL OF THIS

I know this book is jam packed with so many topics that you are not what you signed up for. I know it all seems overwhelming and like it is too much to handle. I know that because that was me too. I thought that it was impossible for me to do all by myself. Truthfully, it was.

I relied heavily on a couple key people, especially in the very early stages. I also learned about all the things that can simplify different tasks. I won't go over them again here, since they are within this book.

If you start with one thing at a time and start chipping away at developing your business and your brand. It will slowly start to come together. It will grow faster than you think it will. Obviously, the more you put in, the more you will get out. Even if you just work at it over time and are not ready to jump in with both feet today, it will happen eventually.

No two companies are the same. No two timelines of how they come about are the same. No two journeys from start to fruition are the same. I wish I could have written this book in the manner of Step 1, Pick a name, Step 2 Buy a Laser, etc. But that is not practical or realistic in any way shape or form.

Every person that reads this book is coming from a different background. All of you are starting with different ideas. And even more so, with different bank accounts backing this up. But that was the whole idea behind writing this book. I wanted all of you to know that it really doesn't matter where you are starting from.

Just start taking the steps that you need to make your dream a reality. It is possible and if you want it enough it can happen. I really hope that after this book is out for a bit, I start seeing more and more laser made crafts.

I hope that some of you set the bar so high that we all are forced to step up our game. The possibilities are endless. Beginning a business this way may lead many of you in many different directions. Some of you may stay small and local. Some of you might branch out and add various other pieces of equipment. Some of you might even become the next household name with the latest and greatest must-have products. If you do, I hope you give a shout out to any help you may have found within these pages.

Thank you, Lisa